DAVID A. HII

MEDIEVAL JEWELLERY

from the eleventh to the fifteenth century

SHIRE ARCHAEOLOGY

TITLES IN THE SHIRE ARCHAEOLOGY SERIES
with their series numbers
Ancient Agricultural Implements Sian E. Rees (15)
Anglo-Saxon Pottery David H. Kennett (5)
Barrows in England and Wales Leslie V. Grinsell (8)
Bronze Age Metalwork in England and Wales Nancy G. Langmaid (4)
Fengate Francis Pryor (20)
Flint Implements of the Old Stone Age Peter Timms (2)
Hillforts of England and Wales James Dyer (16)
Later Stone Implements Michael W. Pitts (14)
Medieval Jewellery David A. Hinton (21)
Medieval Pottery in Britain Jeremy Haslam (6)
Pottery in Roman Britain Vivien G. Swan (3)
Prehistoric Pottery Nancy G. Langmaid (7)
Prehistoric Stone Circles Aubrey Burl (9)
Roman Coinage in Britain P. J. Casey (12)
Roman Roads Richard W. Bagshawe (10)
Roman Villas David E. Johnston (11)
Towns in Roman Britain Julian Bennett (13)
Wood in Archaeology Maisie Taylor (17)

Cover illustration
The Thame ring, largest of the five gold rings
of the Thame hoard. See plates 34-7.
(Ashmolean Museum, Oxford.)

Published by
SHIRE PUBLICATIONS LTD
Cromwell House, Church Street, Princes Risborough,
Aylesbury, Bucks, HP17 9AJ, UK.

Series Editor: James Dyer

ISBN 0 85263 576 1

First published 1982

Printed in Great Britain by
C. I. Thomas & Sons (Haverfordwest) Ltd,
Press Buildings, Merlins Bridge, Haverfordwest.

Contents

Acknowledgements

The plates are reproduced with the permission of the following bodies and institutions: the Trustees of the British Museum, London, plates 1, 6, 8, 9, 12, 13, 19, 23, 26, 27, 31, 33, 41-6; the Visitors of the Ashmolean Museum, Oxford, plates 3, 16, 34-7, 40; Victoria and Albert Museum, Crown Copyright, plates 4, 10, 18, 20, 22, 25, 28, 32; Department of Museum Services, Oxfordshire County Council, plate 15; Birmingham Museums and Art Gallery, plates 17, 39; National Museum of Wales, Cardiff, plate 21; City of Manchester Art Galleries, plate 24; the Trustees, The National Gallery, London, plate 29.

The other photographs were taken by Nick Bradford at the Department of Archaeology, University of Southampton. I am grateful to him for his help and also to all those who lent material that was photographed.

The drawings are by my wife, Susan M. Davies.

I should like to thank the many people who enabled me to collect photographs of objects in the care of their museums and galleries; inevitably some of these pictures have not been used in the publication, but they have nevertheless been of great use to me.

List of plates

1
Introduction

People own jewellery for many reasons: they may want to show off
their wealth; they may admire the fine craftsmanship of the goldsmith
and the silversmith; they may be superstitious and wear jewels as
charms; they may feel that jewellery is a mark of their social status;
they may wear jewels as badges to show where their loyalties lie; or
they may want to convert their money into something that is easily
carried and hidden and provides a convenient way of storing their
wealth. All these motives applied in one way or another in the middle
ages.

Sources of information

Relatively few medieval jewels have survived to this day. Most
would have been melted down when they were no longer wanted by
their owners, the gold and silver to be reworked into some new object,
and the gems to be reset. They were far too valuable simply to throw
away. Nevertheless, even the most precious things can be lost accidentally; one can imagine the household of a rich Southampton
merchant at the end of the twelfth century being turned upside down
while everyone hunted for the valuable gold ring which he had mislaid
(plate 5). But either it had been thrown out by mistake with the
household rubbish, or someone had stolen and hidden it and never
came back to collect it. So it only came to light when archaeologists
were excavating the site of the merchant's house in the 1960s.

Quite often rich people concealed their coins and jewels in a safe
place, intending to return for them later. They could not always do so,
and in rare cases their hoards are found many years later (plates 6, 8,
34, 42-6). Sometimes jewels are kept because they were owned by
someone famous: New College, Oxford, still treasures the jewel bequeathed by the man who founded the college at the end of the
fourteenth century, William of Wykeham (plate 28). Although in
general people were not buried with jewellery and other possessions
after the seventh century, finger rings may be found when the graves
of churchmen are opened, for they were often buried wearing a ring,
frequently the one that they had worn at their consecration (plates 9,
22). Many jewels are found by chance, or their history before they
came into a museum collection may be unknown.

Surviving jewels are not our only evidence. Medieval documents
show that what exists today is only a small fraction of the number of
splendid objects which were owned. For instance, records of her

household expenditure show that Queen Margaret, wife of Henry VI, was a lavish patron of goldsmiths and silversmiths in the middle of the fifteenth century. She was very generous to her servants and to those whose loyalty she wanted to guarantee for the future. Her New Year's Day gifts in 1453 included gold and silver bracelets, rings and collars and individual gems such as a ruby and a diamond, as well as some special things like the sword-belt set with a big diamond, a ruby and two pearls, worth £10, which she gave to Lord Scales, and a 'rose of pure gold', worth 40 shillings, given to Sir Edmund Hull — perhaps this was a little like the pendant found in the contemporary Fishpool hoard (plate 45). Not everyone was as liberal as Queen Margaret; one of her predecessors, Isabella, queen of Edward II, gave her servants annual gifts of money and clothes but seems to have kept for herself the three gold brooches set with rubies and emeralds for which she paid £40 in the year 1311. For members of the royal family, crowns, coronets and diadems were always the biggest items of expenditure.

It was not only royalty who spent large sums on jewels. Lord Fanhope died during the Wars of the Roses owning two brooches worth a staggering £540. Inventories and other records show that many people lower down the social scale had valuable objects. Robberies with violence often involved the theft not only of cash but of jewels, of which the value is usually stated: a gold ring worth 15d was stolen from a man on his way back from Chichester market in 1212; a gold ring set with a ruby worth 40 marks (£26 13s 4d) was taken by a servant from his master in 1220; a gold cross worth two shillings was stolen from a lad who was out in the fields tending his mother's flocks in 1222; a silver clasp worth 7d was reported stolen in 1226 together with cash worth 2s 11d. The import of such luxuries became a source of profit to many merchants, and they are often mentioned in customs records as duty had to be paid on them: for example, an Italian brooch set in the centre with a large pearl surrounded by two sapphires and six rubies was included in the cargo of a ship which landed at Southampton in 1435.

So many people aspired to wear jewels and other expensive things like fur cloaks in the later middle ages that laws were passed intended to force them to have only what was considered appropriate to their status; artisans and yeomen were to own 'no stone nor cloth of silk nor of silver, nor girdle, knife, button, ring, garter, nor ouche (brooch), ribbon, chain, band, seal nor any such other things of gold or of silver'. These laws probably had little effect, but they show that lowly people owned valuables.

Most of these documentary sources are from the later part of the middle ages; there are no comparable records for the eleventh and twelfth centuries. Similarly, another source is only helpful towards the end of the period: sculptures and pictures become increasingly more detailed, and there are portraits, like that of King Richard II (plate 29), which show jewels being worn. Funeral effigies and engraved brasses also provide useful evidence about later medieval fashions. So great was interest in jewels that some were illustrated in the margins of fifteenth-century books, and others were so famous that they were individually named. King Edward I inherited from his father a ring known as 'La Cerise' (The Cherry), presumably because it had a distinctive red stone.

Dating

Few medieval jewels can be dated very exactly. The Southampton gold ring, for instance, is dated to the late twelfth century because it was found with pottery and other objects of that date in a pit which had been filled and sealed some time before a stone house was built above it in the thirteenth century. Dating by association is important when hoards of jewellery are considered: the two silver brooches from Coventry (plate 8) were found with coins of which the latest was minted just before 1298. The brooches may not have been brand new when they were hidden, but it is unlikely that they were 'antiques', so they were probably made in the second half of the thirteenth century. Walter de Gray was Archbishop of York from 1215 to 1255; the ring found in his tomb (plate 9) should therefore date to the early thirteenth century. Similarly, Archbishop Geoffrey de Ludham's must have been made before 1265 (also plate 9).

There are not many jewels that can be dated because of their context or because their owner is someone whose name is recorded in a historical document. Usually dating is by comparison; the object is like one whose date is known, or there is a picture of one very like it in an illustration such as the panel painting of King Richard II shown on plate 29. If the jewel has an inscription (plates 25, 34, 43), the style of the letters provides a further clue. Stylistic dating of this sort depends on personal judgement and is less reliable than dating by context.

The smiths

The men who made medieval jewels had to be both very skilled and very rich, as they had to have valuable stocks of gold, silver and gems. In eleventh-century England many were also responsible for minting coins, but this became a separate activity as the number of towns which were mint centres declined, and the production of coinage was increasingly concentrated on the Tower at London.

In documentary sources jewellers and moneyers are usually called goldsmiths *(aurifabri)* since their main trade was in the making of gold and silver plate, rather than jewels, both for church and domestic use. Cups, dishes, drinking horns and other vessels might be studded with gems, in settings very like those used in jewellery. For the Church, elaborate shrines, crosses and statues were made. The smiths had to have very secure premises in which to keep their stock, and their houses were often among the first to be built of stone in twelfth-century towns, stone walls and clay roof tiles being less vulnerable to fire than timber and thatch. In towns like Canterbury and Winchester their houses and workshops were in the streets where rents were highest and the most important people lived. Many goldsmiths served as borough officials, their wealth making them prominent in civic affairs.

In western Europe the great centre of goldworking was Paris, and many of the most famous jewellers worked there; the records contain many references to purchases by English royalty from French smiths. England's constant involvement in France and the close ties between the two countries meant that the English usually looked to Paris as the arbiter of taste and fashion, although purchases were also made from Italian merchants and occasionally from Flanders and Spain. In the fourteenth and fifteenth centuries the patronage of the Dukes of Burgundy made that area even more famous than Paris, and jewels found in England have been attributed to Burgundian workmanship (plates 34, 39).

2
Materials

Metals

Gold had to be imported into western Europe. The nearest source was Bohemia, but the mines there did not become significant producers until the late middle ages, when improved drainage techniques made it possible to work deeper lodes. The supplies on which Europe relied came from Arabian merchants, usually trading with Italians from Venice and other cities. Some came through Spain, where the Moors acted as dealers. The metal came from the mines in Persia and beyond, or from Africa, being shipped up the east coast or brought on caravans across the Sahara.

Gold is a hard metal, so that very delicate patterns can be cut into it. It becomes malleable if gently heated, so that very fine wires *(filigree)* can be formed. A rod of gold is rolled out and then its diameter is reduced by pulling it through a hole in a steel drawbar, the operation being repeated with successively smaller holes. If the tongs holding the end of the wire are turned while the gold is being pulled through, a twisted wire will result. If this is done with base metals they will almost invariably crack or spring back, but gold if properly handled will hold its shape. Mercury flux is used as a solder to secure the filigree to a backplate and to join different pieces together (plate 37). Gold can be cut or punched; if cut right through, it is called *openwork* (plates 35, 39). *Engraving* removes some of the gold from the surface (plate 12); *tracing* or *chasing* is the scoring of a very fine line, so that none of the metal is removed. An all-over pattern of fine dots punched into the surface is called *pointillé* work. Less handwork is needed if the gold is cast in a mould. Coin designs are hammered *(struck)* on to a blank flan, but this technique is not appropriate in jewellery. The final operation was the polishing of the gold.

Silver is found in England in the same deposits as lead, in the Mendips and Cumbria. The technology of separating the ores was probably not known, however, and is in any case too costly to be worth implementing. Most silver came from Saxony, and later from Bohemia, much of it as foreign coins, which were then melted down. The relative value of gold to silver fluctuated between about eight and ten to one.

Silver is a much softer metal than gold, so cannot be used for such fine work, although the same processes can be applied. A thin film of gold leaf can be coated on to the surface of silver by using mercury *(gilding),* but the gilt soon wears off if the object is used or polished very much. By gilding some parts and not others a contrast in colours can be achieved.

Bronze (copper alloy) is a base metal which cannot be worked as finely as gold or silver, though a skilled mouldmaker can do good cast work (plate 3). Gold rings, brooches and other fashionable jewels were often copied in bronze, glass and coloured pastes being used instead of gems (plate 14).

Pewter is an alloy of lead and tin. England was Europe's principal source for tin, from the deposits in west Devon and east Cornwall. Pewter plates and other vessels were common in England and were regarded by foreign visitors as a sign of the country's wealth. A few pewter jewels were made, mostly in the eleventh century and earlier. The metal is too soft to be skilfully worked and does not harden, so that it cannot stand up to much use. It was, however, the metal from which pilgrims' badges were mass-produced in stone moulds (plate 38).

Tin is used in pewter but was also used for *tinning* iron or bronze so that they might be mistaken for silver. The process was used on spurs and is sometimes seen on bronze brooches but does not seem to have been popular otherwise.

Gemstones

Diamonds did not circulate in western Europe until the fourteenth century, when the art of cutting them seems to have been learnt, first by Italians, and then by craftsmen at Paris and other centres. No example of a jewel set with a diamond is known to have survived from England (a gold ring, recently discovered on an excavation in Lancashire, is reported to have an uncut diamond in it, though this remains to be substantiated), but *The Black Prince's Register* shows that by the 1350s there were diamonds in the royal treasury. In 1352 the Prince's sister-in-law was given 'an ouch (clasp or brooch, from the Italian *nocchia*) set with . . . two diamonds at the sides . . . and two diamonds in the middle', and rings set with diamonds were given to various gentlemen of the household. In 1355 a merchant of 'Gyene' (possibly Genoa) was paid £70 for an 'eastern ruby and a great diamond'. Thereafter references become more frequent; in 1461, the Duke of York is recorded as having pledged to Sir John Fastolf jewels which included a brooch 'with a great pointed diamond', a clear indication that the gem had been skilfully cut. Another royal jewel set with diamonds was described as a 'feterlock' — presumably an object like the padlock from the Fishpool hoard (plates 42, 43; another 'fetirlock' was owned in 1463 by John Baret, a merchant of Bury St Edmunds).

Rubies were much more common than diamonds and like most gems were cabochons, i.e. they had a rounded top and a flat bottom and were circular or oval rather than square or rectangular, avoiding the need for cutting (plate 12). They came to Europe from India, Ceylon and Burma, and there are also many references to 'baleys' or 'balas rubies'. These ought to be spinels, red stones from Afghanistan from geological deposits which also yield rubies, but it is very doubtful if the distinction between spinels and rubies was known in the west.

The later medieval skill in gem cutting can be seen in the ruby in the centre of the stem of the New College jewel (plate 28).

Sapphires were regarded as particularly appropriate for the rings worn by churchmen. All stones had magical properties ascribed to them, and books known as lapidaries described what the stones could do for their owners: sapphires helped them to concentrate their minds on the heavenly kingdom but also relieved them from the sweating sickness and, if the worst came to the worst, helped them to escape from prison! Such superstitions were not condemned by the Church as it was believed that the stones' properties were part of the natural order, and thus of God's creation. In 1219 a legal action was necessary to recover three gold rings, one of which contained a sapphire, from a woman who had borrowed them when she was sick, presumably in the belief that they would help to cure her. Such stories show how the stones were put to practical use. A sadder record is of the disappearance of a boy in 1221 who had worn a ring round his neck in the hope that it would improve his bad eye. Typically, he enters the historical record not because of an investigation into his suspected murder, but because of a dispute over the custody of his property.

The source of sapphires was Ceylon; that was where the stone in Archbishop Walter de Gray's ring came from (plate 9). The gem is large enough to reveal a distinctive mineralogical pattern under a high-powered microscope. Most medieval stones are too small to be traced accurately to source in this way.

Garnets and **amethysts** are red like rubies and may sometimes have been passed off as the more precious stone — there seem to be more references in medieval documents to rubies than might be expected. Garnet is only a semiprecious stone and probably came from Bohemia. Amethyst is a superior stone; its properties were the comfort of the body and soul, success in the hunting field and the cure of hangovers.

Both sapphires and amethysts were sometimes *faceted*, i.e. the sides and top were cut to flat surfaces. The art of this sort of cutting was known at a much earlier date than was that of cutting diamonds and is found in twelfth-century jewels (plate 4). Improved late medieval skills account for the cutting of the amethysts on the Thame ring (plates 34-7 and cover), particularly the complicated double cross on the front.

Pearls cannot be shaped, although they can be pierced for wearing as beads or on dowels (plate 33). Strictly speaking, they are not gems, since they are organic, growing in oysters and mussels. As the Venetian ambassador noted in his despatches home at the end of the fifteenth century, England produced her own seed pearls, but they were very small ones, and larger ones had to come from the Orient, from the Persian Gulf and the Red Sea. Pearls were often sewn on to costume, so they are recorded in their hundreds in medieval inventories, where they are often called *marguerites*.

From the same waters as large pearls came **coral,** particularly favoured for rosary beads (Chaucer's Prioress had a pair of them on a bracelet), perhaps because, being red, coral was the colour of Christ's blood.

Toadstones were so called because they were thought to come from inside the head of a toad, although they are actually fossilised fish teeth. Although a dull, off-white opaque colour, they were quite widely worn as an antidote to poison.

Cameos were very rare and highly treasured. To make one, a stone with two colours occurring in it in bands, such as onyx, is required. One colour is left as the background while the overlying band, usually white, is cut to create a relief design. This is extremely skilled work and was not known in the middle ages until the Italians revived the craft in the fourteenth century. The Oxwich brooch (plate 21) is a very early example of this revival. Most medieval examples were classical gems reused. They were particularly sought after for use on shrines and other church treasures but were increasingly used on secular jewellery. Henry III, who was a lavish purchaser of jewels, paid £93 6s 8d for one cameo in 1255 and £100 for another from a Cologne goldsmith. He originally offered only 100 marks (£66 13s 4d) for the second but had to pay the higher sum 'with all speed' to complete the deal. That cameo was given to the shrine of St Edward at Westminster, one of many such donations which benefited religious houses that cared for the relics of favoured saints.

Engraved gems were also highly valued classical survivals. Although the engraving technique is described in the widely circulated treatise *Diversarum Artium Schedula* written by a twelfth-century monk, Theophilus, it was probably not much before the end of the thirteenth century that Italian craftsmen revived its practice. Classical gems were set in medieval jewels (plate 20), however, and devices on gold seals (e.g. on rings, plate 10) show that they were an important influence on that aspect of design.

Other materials

Jet is found in the Whitby area of North Yorkshire and was used occasionally in medieval jewellery for beads, small crucifix pendants and buttons. Being black, unlike any other natural mineral in Europe, it was particularly suitable for devotional objects such as paternoster beads but was not used in rings and brooches.

Enamel is basically coloured glass and is the medium through which a wide range of different hues can be added to gold and silver. Usually this is done by filling hollowed-out compartments in the design with a paste of coloured glass mixed with water and heating it very gently so that the paste fuses with the background. The enamel can then be polished. By the fourteenth and fifteenth centuries skilful workers had learnt how to cover a complete surface with different enamels without having a strip of metal between each. Another late use of the medium was to cover a surface with opaque enamel, a technique especially suitable for three-dimensional work (e.g. the Dunstable swan, plate 31), and too difficult to be widely practised, because of the need to prevent the enamel from flaking off.

Niello is applied to jewels in the same way as enamel and is a metallic sulphide. It provided the closest to black in colour that a medieval jeweller could achieve and was thus a popular background on gold and silver objects, as the sparkling metal is shown off to best effect against the contrasting dark niello (plate 8). Black enamel was sometimes used as an alternative to niello in the fourteenth and fifteenth centuries (plate 32) but was less suitable because it was more liable to flake.

3
Types of jewel

Finger rings

The hoop of a finger ring does not require much gold or silver, and this is one reason for the widespread use of rings. In the eleventh century rings seem to have consisted of plaits of straight or tapering wires (plate 1) or plain bands with overlapping ends, often crudely stamped. Rings set with gems were worn by churchmen in such ceremonies as consecration services, and they often have very wide hoops so that they could be worn over gloves. Bishops' rings were blessed by the Pope. When a bishop died, some of his rings were supposed to go to the king as a form of tax payment, but one ring was usually buried with him. Twelfth-century examples from Durham include those found in the tombs of Ranulph Flambard, who died in 1128, and William de St Barbe (plate 4).

A finger-ring shape which was introduced probably around the middle of the twelfth century and remained popular until the fifteenth had a stirrup-shaped hoop of gold set with a single stone almost enclosed in the gold (plates 15, 16). If the stone was a large one, it might be held in a scalloped setting (plate 34) or by small gold *claws* (plate 18). By the end of the twelfth century rings became available which had a large central stone surrounded by smaller ones (plate 9). The hoops of rings might also be decorated by simple faceting so that the gold caught the light (plate 5), or by the fourteenth century the shoulder of the ring might be engraved with sprays of flowers and other patterns (plate 46), and sometimes these engravings would be filled with coloured enamels; unfortunately few examples of this survive, because the enamel did not adhere firmly to the gold and tended to fall out. There are a few finger rings in which the hoop is very finely worked into the bodies of fantastic creatures, which hold the bezel in their front legs (plate 39).

Although many of the most splendid rings were owned by ecclesiastics, they also became popular with the laity. The late twelfth-century ring from Southampton (plate 5) shows that a rich merchant might by then aspire to wear something more elaborate than a simple gold band. The six rings (plate 6) found in a hoard at Worcester with coins dated to *c.* 1180 show the range already available, if the context is reliable. The three rings with square, faceted bezels belong in the twelfth century, as we have seen from the Durham rings, but the plaited wire ring may have been a century old by 1180, and the other two seem more likely to be of thirteenth-century than twelfth-century workmanship. A brooch ascribed to the same hoard also seems out of place in the late twelfth century.

One of the Worcester ring hoops is in the shape of two clasped hands and is an example of a *love ring,* given at a marriage betrothal or for similar romantic reasons. *Posy rings* also came into fashion: these were inscribed with mottoes or rhymes, usually in French, which was considered the courtly language. *Je suis ici en lieu d'ami* ('I am here in a friend's place') was a favourite motto on a present to a loved one. Often the inscription was on the inside of the hoop of the ring, as though to keep it a secret between giver and wearer, and the outside was decorated with flowers (plate 34). Another kind of love ring had twin bezels, to symbolise the two lovers side by side (plate 26). All this conforms to the romantic tradition of courtly love fostered in the thirteenth and fourteenth centuries.

More practical were signet rings, in which the bezel was engraved with its owner's device, so that it could be used for sealing documents (plates 10, 11). By the end of the thirteenth century even peasants at the bottom of the social scale were supposed to have their own seals, showing how important correct legal procedures had become. It is not surprising therefore that there are many signet rings and that many of them are in base metals. Rings are often recorded as being sent with messages, as proof of authenticity. A signet ring would be particularly appropriate for this, which may be another reason for the relatively large number of base metal ones that are known. It is sometimes said that this is because of the effect of the sumptuary laws in the mid fourteenth century, but the increase seems to predate these.

Other rings with inscriptions include mourning rings, fashionable in the fourteenth century and later. In 1463 John Baret bequeathed to a local friend 'a double ring with a ruby and a turquoise, with a scripture written within, for a remembrance of old love virtuously set at all times to the pleasure of God'. Rings with cabalistic or astrological words show contemporary interest in alchemy. Commonest were religious inscriptions, for which Latin was usual, *Ave Maria plena gracia* being the most popular. Often such rings were engraved with figures of saints or apostles, these devotional rings being worn by both priests and laity (plate 40). Baret bequeathed a ring 'with an image of the Trinity' to his wife. An outstanding example is the Thame ring, with its relic casket (plate 34). Rings might also have a protective role, through the gems in their bezels, or by inscription or association. Baret had 'a cramp ring with black enamel and part silver and gilt', a cramp ring being one which preserved the owner from fits and had been blessed by the king or queen at a special Good Friday ceremony.

Brooches

Unlike finger rings, a few elaborate eleventh-century brooches are known (plate 2). They continued the Anglo-Saxon disc-brooch tradition and were held in place by a pin at the back which swivelled on a projecting hinge and fitted into a catch.

Brooches do not seem to have been worn to any great extent during the twelfth century, probably because the rather heavy dress worn did not call for delicate jewellery. During the thirteenth century, however, costume fashions altered and brooches were again in demand. Nearly all were ring brooches, being circles rather than discs, with a constriction at one point on the circumference where the pin swivelled (plate 8). There was no catch to hold the pin, which was held in place simply by the pull of the material through which it was pushed. Both the pins and the circles could be decorated, with inscriptions, gems or bosses. The inscriptions, like those on the finger rings, might be religious, amatory or magical. They were worn by both men and women.

The simple circle of the ring brooch could easily be adapted to a variety of different shapes. Some were hexagons or octagons: others were a series of joined circles. Some of the prettiest are heart-shaped (plate 42). Even more elaborate brooches might take the form of human, animal or bird bodies joined to make a continuous circle. Hands held out in prayer were a popular motif. Such brooches were not only worn by the rich aristocracy; thousands were made in bronze, often set with glass or paste beads where a finer brooch would have had a gem.

The popularity of the brooch and the elaboration of its design eventually led to the production of brooches which again had a hinged pin and catch on the back. The Founder's Jewel in New College, Oxford (plate 28), is a late fourteenth-century brooch shaped as a letter M, the initial of Mary, mother of God and patron saint of the college. The brooch worn by the Prioress in Chaucer's *Canterbury Tales,* which was written at much the same time as New College was founded, was probably in the shape of a letter A, and on it was the inscription *Amor vincit omnia* ('Love conquers all'), a very popular text. Wheel-shaped and disc-shaped brooches were also worn, embellished with very elaborate settings of gems and goldwork. Others might be badges (see below).

A brooch is an ornament that can be worn just as decoration or can be used as a clasp to hold clothes together. The ring brooches were more often functional than the brooches with pins on the back, which could stand only light pressure. Similarly there is often little distinction between a ring brooch and a buckle; many plain circular buckles were worn in the later middle ages to hold up men's hose and breeches (plate 30).

Belt and costume fittings

An important item of medieval clothing for both men and women was the belt, and many very expensively decorated ones are recorded in documents; unfortunately the leather or textile of which they were made rarely survives, unlike the more durable metal buckles, strap ends and mounts with which they were embellished. The surviving English examples are mostly of bronze, worn mainly by the lower social ranks (plate 30).

Some eleventh-century and twelfth-century buckles and strap ends (which prevented the end of the belt from fraying) are in cast bronze, with animal or plant patterns: the frame of a buckle might be a pair of stylised animals back to back, or a strap end might be an openwork frieze with animals, birds and plants (plate 3). This interest in three-dimensional designs does not seem to have lasted beyond the twelfth century. Some bone buckles were also made, but they too ceased to be common.

Elaborate fittings were the minority, however, and most twelfth-century buckles were either plain or decorated only with simple notches. From these straightforward shapes there evolved during the thirteenth century buckles with wider frames, and these might be engraved or in rare cases enamelled. Often a metal plate was added; the buckle swivelled on this, and the belt was sewn or riveted to the plate, not folded over the back of the frame of the buckle (plate 30). The plate gave scope for a wide range of engraved ornament, and this too might occasionally be enamelled. The vogue for this ornament seems to have ended during the fourteenth century, but the fifteenth century saw a revival of ornamentation, this time with very large, solid or openwork buckle plates and strap ends, sometimes with religious motifs. Sometimes strap ends of this sort ended in a loop or a hook, an alternative method of fastening a belt if it does not have to fit tightly: those with hooks were often used to clip into a loop on a sword scabbard.

The great majority of buckles were not embellished, however; for everyday costume a plain buckle was enough. In the fourteenth century the double-frame *spectacle* buckle was introduced, with the strap fitted on to the central bar. Rectangular buckles usually belong to the fifteenth century and later. Large iron buckles were for harness rather than costume use.

A curious male fashion in the late fourteenth and fifteenth centuries was the wearing of small bells on a sash. This probably accounts for many of the small bronze bells which are found (plate 30), though others would have been on hounds' collars or hawks' legs. Bells are referred to in such records as the inventory of the property of the widow of Sir William Windsor made in 1378, which included 'collars with cokebells of silver'.

Badges

Hat and other badges were worn in the later middle ages to show allegiance to the king or to one of the great noble families. King Richard II's badge was the chained hart (plate 29), and Henry IV, who usurped his throne, had a chained swan as one of the Lancastrian emblems (plate 31). A different sort of badge was the pewter one worn by a pilgrim (plate 38).

Pendants and necklaces

Fifteenth-century female costume left the throat and neck bare, so that necklaces were particularly appropriate as an accessory, although there are plenty of earlier references to them. A pendant provided a striking centrepiece: this might be a gem or a badge (plate 45), but a cross seems to have been the most popular (plate 33), reflecting the conventional piety of the late middle ages, as do strings of rosary beads. Complete necklaces have not survived. The long gold chains in the Fishpool hoard may have been for use as necklaces (plate 44), but they do not have attachments and may have been used to hold together the two hems of a cloak, worn open across the front of the body.

Crowns and coronets

The greatest efforts of the jewellers were expended on objects that have not survived in England, and written descriptions and pictures (plate 29) are the only source of information on the diadems, crowns and coronets worn on state occasions. Such items were usually made by a goldsmith from stock supplied to him for the purpose, rather than being bought ready made, but in 1253 Henry III paid 500 marks (£333 13s 4d) for a crown bought from a foreign merchant. In 1269 40 shillings wages were paid to 'those who repaired the king's crown', but we are not told which crown this was.

Knives and weapons

Almost everybody carried a knife, to cut meat or to use in self defence as need arose. Daggers were also very common, and swords were often carried, not only on ceremonial occasions. It is surprising therefore that the handles of these weapons were not elaborately decorated, as they had been in the Anglo-Saxon period. Sword pommels, for instance, were rarely more than cast bronze terminals, in various different shapes, but not set with gold or silver panels. The weight of the pommel was important, to balance the weapon when it was swung, but the bronze was not usually even simply enamelled. Very occasionally, a late medieval sword or dagger might have gems set in its grip. Leather scabbards had quite elaborate ornament impressed on to them and might have bronze mounts; chapes from the ends of scabbards are often found.

Knife blades in the eleventh and twelfth centuries sometimes had strips of silver or copper inlaid into their surfaces, in lines or scroll patterns. But this technique did not remain popular.

Harness

Horses are as much a status symbol as clothes and at tournaments or in the field of battle they were richly decked out with brightly coloured cloths, as well as with protective armour. The most common survival of harness decoration is a small bronze pendant, often shield-shaped and bearing the owner's coat of arms or that of his liege lord. These were usually enamelled and were attached to the harness on the horse's head.

Stirrups in the eleventh and twelfth centuries might be inlaid with metal strips of contrasting colour, like contemporary knife blades, or the iron might be encased in bronze sheets. Iron spurs were often *fusion-plated* with a very thin coating of tin, so that they flashed in the light. Bronze spurs were much less common: these might be gilded.

4
Jewellery and history

As we have seen, the use of jewellery is part of social and economic history. It shows people's wealth and aspirations, the importance of rank in society and the skill of the best craftsmen. If we are to use jewellery as evidence to help us to understand the history of the middle ages, we have to be aware of the limitations of our knowledge, such as the more ample documentary records that we have for the fourteenth and fifteenth centuries than exist for the eleventh and twelfth centuries.

It is probable that precious metals had been much more important to the Anglo-Saxons than they were to Englishmen in the eleventh and twelfth centuries. The plain finger rings and the relative absence of brooches show that jewellery was not then held in high regard. Although there were plenty of goldsmiths, they were employed in making goblets and other tableware and church plate, rather than personal ornaments.

The second half of the twelfth century probably saw the beginning of a marked change. The Southampton merchant's ring is an example (plate 5), but we have to look to France to see brooches coming back into fashion. Inflation may have played a part; rising prices probably show that more precious metals were available than before, and jewellery may have been a better long-term investment than coin. Henry III's French wife and his own artistic interests may have spread new fashions, but there is a sad lack of evidence for the thirteenth century generally. The two Coventry ring brooches (plate 8) do however suggest that such things were relatively common by 1300.

The fourteenth and fifteenth centuries provide us with most of our evidence. It seems that jewellery was once again an important status symbol, and costumes were worn, by both men and women, which showed it to good effect. The garments themselves were often heavily encrusted with gems and pearls, edged with gold thread and embroidered with patterns that occurred also on the jewels. Large amounts of money were spent.

Anyone living in the late middle ages was aware of more than just a life of luxury and lavish display, however. It was a time of plague and sudden death. Reliquaries and magical stones were worn to stave off unseen perils, as well as for a show of simple piety. It was also a time of violence, and it was good sense to convert wealth into jewels which could be pawned in time of need. Land, although still of the first importance, was slightly less attractive at a time when a man who supported the loser in a battle could have his estates taken from him by an angry king; jewels could be taken into exile. The Fishpool hoard (plates 42-6) may have been owned by someone who hid it while fleeing from pursuit after unsuccessful efforts by the Lancastrians to oust the Yorkist kings. The Thame hoard (plates 34-7) is contemporary with it, and its deposition may have some similar dark story behind it. Even the exquisite Dunstable swan (plate 31) is a symbol of men's needs to show their loyalties and the difficulties that making the wrong choice entailed.

Lavish display was a sign of great wealth, but it was facilitated by the more ready availability of gold. Enough gold was circulating in England for it to be used to mint high value coins after 1343, instead of silver. To prevent those of lower rank from imitating their social superiors, sumptuary laws set out what was seemly for each class to wear. Superficially this was good for the realm, for the laws were meant to stop people from squandering their goods so that they could not 'help their liege lord' in his time of need. But behind this may have been the problem of the fluidity of the social structure; great families could die out very quickly, and there was no security even in the royal dynasty. Was the late medieval legislation which set out to restrict the lesser knights and the bourgeoisie a sign of the aristocracy's uncertainty of its own tenure? Perhaps the jewellery should not be seen so much as a mark of wealth and display as one of insecurity and doubt.

Note

Anyone reading this book will appreciate that jewellery is an important source of social history. The discovery of new pieces is one of the ways in which we learn more about this, but such finds are only fully understood if the context from which they came is known. A ring found in a rubbish pit in a medieval town tells us about the life of the townsmen as well as about the history of jewellery; a hoard is only useful if we know everything about it — not only the coins and jewels, but the pot or bag in which they were found, and the exact place in which it was concealed. It is very sad that in the last few years the practice of treasure hunting has been revived in Britain, usually by means of metal detectors. Irresponsible use of these has led to objects being removed from their contexts in the ground without any thought for the information that is being destroyed in the process. Nor does the damage stop there; ignorance too often leads to destruction of the objects. A vigorous wipe of a surface is often enough to remove delicate enamel from its background; rough handling can scratch a surface; washing can dissolve the last of an adhesive that was holding a gem tenuously into a setting. Skilled conservation is necessary if things are to survive exposure. (I once had brought to me for identification an object which the finder had 'cleaned' with the point of a needle; the idiot had picked out all the niello inlay from a gold ring, thinking that it was just dirt!).

The study of jewellery, like the study of any other aspect of archaeology, is not 'the indulging of a craving acquisitiveness and the adornment of glass cases with ill understood relics' (Charles Warne, 1846) but leads to greater knowledge and understanding of our history. Nothing which does not further that aim should be tolerated.

Museums to visit

The best collections of medieval jewellery are in London. The **British Museum** has the Waddesdon Bequest and many other fine pieces. The museum has the great advantage that items declared treasure trove are offered to it by the Crown. The recently discovered Fishpool hoard was therefore acquired by it, although the hoard was found in Nottinghamshire. Its policy is to display together all its items from a historical period, so that the visitor gets an overall picture of medieval culture. The opposite approach is taken by the **Victoria and Albert Museum**, which displays all its jewellery from all periods and places in one gallery. This allows the visitor to compare the different ways in which jewellery has been made throughout history (although the effect can be overpowering). The **Museum of London**, in the heart of the city, has some very good pieces, shown in their social context of the life of the capital.

Outside London, there is no single comprehensive collection. There is a good collection of finger rings at the **Ashmolean Museum** in Oxford, where the Thame hoard is kept. A large selection of base metal objects is shown, giving a better idea of the total production of the middle ages than most museums do. The **National Museum of Wales** at Cardiff has a good display of objects found in the Principality. **Birmingham City Museum** has some interesting pieces. Other museums often have one or two examples of jewellery, but the **National Museum of Antiquities of Scotland** at Edinburgh is the only other in Britain to have a large holding.

Further reading

Evans, Joan. *A History of Jewellery, 1100-1870.* Faber and Faber, London, revised edition 1970. The best general introduction to the subject, dealing with European jewellery as a whole, though best on French and English work. Well illustrated, with some colour plates.

Oman, C. *British Rings, 800-1914.* Batsford, London, 1974. The first survey of a particular topic. Magisterial, though very readable. Better on the post-Conquest than the pre-Conquest period. Very good black and white photographs, less good colour plates.

Rudoe, Judy. *Medieval Jewellery.* British Museum Publications Ltd, London, 1976. A short introduction to a wallet of twelve excellent colour slides from the British Museum's collection.

London Museum. *Medieval Catalogue.* 1940, frequently reprinted. Basic introduction to the whole range of medieval artefacts, especially good on everyday objects such as buckles, strap ends etc.

Cherry, J. 'The Dunstable Swan Jewel'. *Journal of the British Archaeological Association,* volume 32, 1969. The comprehensive study of this outstanding find.

Cherry, J. 'The Medieval Jewellery from the Fishpool, Nottinghamshire, Hoard'. *Archaeologia,* volume 104, 1973. Full details about this important discovery.

Evans, Joan and Serjeantson, Mary S. *English Medieval Lapidaries.* Early English Texts Society, London, 1933. Edited texts of these fascinating documents.

Jessup, R. *Anglo-Saxon Jewellery.* Shire Publications, Aylesbury, 1975. The companion book to this one, dealing with the pre-Conquest period.

 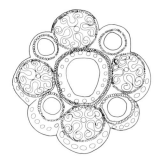

Plate 1 (left). Gold finger ring, made of plaited wires, the ends of which are beaten together at the back of the hoop. Rings like this date to the tenth and eleventh centuries, and many have been found, both in gold and in silver. Some of bracelet size are also known. This one was excavated in Oxford and shows the town's prosperity in the late Saxon period. (On loan from the British Museum, London, to the Oxford City Museum. Twice actual size.)

Plate 2 (right). A gold brooch, found in London with eleventh-century coins, made of twisted wires and set with a central sapphire surrounded by pearls. Unfortunately the brooch has not survived and is only known from an eighteenth-century drawing.

Plate 3. Cast bronze strap ends were popular in the tenth and eleventh centuries. This example is from Ixworth, Suffolk; the drawing clarifies its details. It has a central plant stem and there is a bird on each side. (Ashmolean Museum, Oxford. Actual size.)

Plate 4 (left). Gold finger ring of William de St Barbe (or Barbara), Bishop of Durham, who died in 1158. It was found in his grave in the chapter house. In the bezel is a large sapphire cut into octagonal facets. (Now in the Cathedral Museum, Durham. Photograph by Victoria and Albert Museum, London. Twice actual size.)

Plate 5 (right). Gold finger ring, set with three rounded and polished garnets, the hoop cut and notched to make the gold catch the light. It was found in a late twelfth-century rubbish pit in Southampton. At that time the port's trade was thriving, bringing wealth to its merchants and citizens, one of whom presumably lost this precious ring. (God's House Tower Museum, Southampton. Twice actual size.)

Plate 6. Six of the seven finger rings found at Worcester with a hoard of coins, the latest of which dated to *c.* 1180. All those shown are of silver (the seventh is bronze and is similar to the top row, centre). The three on the bottom row have amethyst, crystal and yellow paste settings respectively, with notching on the shoulders. Top row, left, has ornamental panels with crosses and chequers; top centre is probably earlier in date than the rest (compare plate 1); top right is cut to look like a pair of clasped hands (compare plate 14). It is interesting to see the range of different ring designs which were already available by the end of the twelfth century. (Now in the British Museum).

Plate 7. Silver-gilt brooch with elaborate filigree decoration (i.e. twisted wires) and pellets, soldered to a backplate. It was probably made in the Rhineland — yet it was found in a disused pottery kiln at Laverstock, Wiltshire! How such a precious object could have reached this resting place fifty years or more after it was made is unknown; the potters would surely not have been rich enough to own it, and their workshop would not have been the sort of place normally visited by wealthy patrons. (Salisbury and South Wiltshire Museum. Twice actual size.)

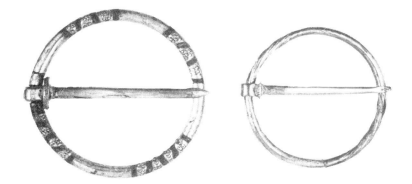

Plate 8. Two silver ring brooches, found in Coventry with coins dated to *c.* 1298. The frames are rings of silver wire. The larger has panels of stamped circles set off by black niello fused into grooves. The smaller has two quadrants which have been twisted to contrast with the other two, which have been left plain. (British Museum. Actual size.)

Plate 9. Gold finger rings found in the coffins of two of the Archbishops of York, revealed during restoration of the Minster in 1968. At the top are two views of the ring of Godfrey de Ludham (died 1265): a sapphire is held in place by four small gold claws. The hoop is stirrup-shaped, a grand version of a very popular type (compare plates 15 and 16). Below is the magnificent ring buried with Archbishop Walter de Gray in 1255; he was one of the most important men in England, and his ring reflects his status. It has a sapphire in a claw setting, surrounded by rubies and emeralds, another popular design (compare plates 17 and 18). (Now in York Minster Crypt. Photographs by British Museum, Actual size.)

Plate 10. Two gold finger rings engraved on the bezels so that they could be used as seals. Signet rings like these were very common. The devices on the bezels of these two examples suggest that they were merchants' rings, for similar designs were often used as marks to authenticate the ownership of merchandise traded from place to place. It is not usually possible to ascribe them to an owner who is known from other sources, as they were not legally validated, and so there is no way of knowing which merchant used a particular device. (Victoria and Albert Museum. Twice actual size.)

Plate 11. Bronze signet ring engraved with a very simple device of a cross and dots. By the fourteenth century even quite poor people might have to have a seal, for legal documents, so base metal seals like this are often found. This one was excavated recently at Christchurch Priory, Dorset. (Twice actual size.)

Plate 12. Gold ring brooch, at the top of which two hands protrude and clasp an opal. At the bottom is a ruby in a gold collar, and there are two gold studs cut into Gothic leaf patterns. Around the ring is engraved the inscription *AVE MARIA G,* the *G* being an abbreviation for *gracia plena* ('Hail Mary, full of grace'). The devotional text shows that the hands are to be interpreted as being clasped in prayer. Late thirteenth or fourteenth century. (British Museum. Twice actual size.)

Plate 13 (left). The motif of clasped hands is used on this gold finger ring as a symbol of its donor's love for its fortunate recipient. An inscription runs round the hoop; in the part visible in the photograph, the letter on the far left is an N, accidentally engraved back to front, suggesting that the craftsman was illiterate. Rings like this might be given at betrothal or marriage. This one was found in London. (British Museum. Actual size.)

Plate 14 (right). Another love ring, having the clasped hands as parts of the hoop. Such *fede* rings (from the Latin word for faith) were very popular, as this example shows, since it is in bronze gilded to gleam like gold. It was clearly designed for a mass market, not made for a rich patron like those in gold or silver (compare plate 6). (Excavated at Christchurch Priory, Dorset. Actual size.)

Plate 15 (left). A gold finger ring excavated recently at the site of the Blackfriars in Oxford. The stone in the bezel is a small sapphire. Rings like this were often worn by members of the ecclesiastical orders as well as by the laity and it is especially interesting that this example was found in a friary, since the brothers were supposed to have no worldly goods. It might have been dropped by a visitor, but it was discovered in a part of the establishment where visitors would not normally have gone, so much more probably it illustrates a lowering of standards in the fourteenth century. (Now in the Oxford City Museum. Actual size.)

Plate 16 (right). A side view of another ring very like that in plate 15, to show the full profile of such 'stirrup-shaped' rings (compare plate 9). This one is also in gold, but many base metal examples are known. They first appeared in the twelfth century — possibly even in the eleventh — and were probably still worn in the fifteenth. (Ashmolean Museum, Oxford. Actual size.)

Plate 17 (left). Gold finger ring, having a central sapphire cut into an irregular hexagon, surrounded by two small diamonds and two rubies in projecting settings. Such clustering of stones was favoured (compare plate 9) despite the risk of damage to the precariously mounted subsidiary gems. (Found at Mansfield Woodhouse, Nottinghamshire. Now in Birmingham City Museum. Actual size.)

Plate 18 (right). Another example of a gold ring which has a cluster of small stones, in this case amethysts, round the centre. The big sapphire is held in place by four small gold claws (compare plate 9), in each of which is set a tiny gem. (Found at Epsom, Surrey. Now in the Victoria and Albert Museum. Actual size.)

Plate 19. Another way in which several stones could be set in a single ring is shown here. The larger stones are an amethyst and a sapphire, and the two smaller ones are turquoises. Filigree bands between them would help to catch the light. This ring was found in London and can be compared in design to that excavated recently in Southampton (plate 5). (British Museum. Twice actual size.)

Plate 20. Gemstones taken from classical jewellery were much admired and were reset in medieval rings, brooches and church ornaments. In this finger ring of the thirteenth or fourteenth century found at Witney, Oxfordshire, the hoop is a thin band of gold, and the gem is held in place by four claws. The classical stone is an intricately cut female bust, which is shown in the drawing for clarity. (Victoria and Albert Museum. Actual size.)

Plate 21. This magnificent ring brooch (its pin is missing) was found at Oxwich Castle, West Glamorgan, and illustrates the popularity of another classical gem, the cameo. Here three male busts, set in oval frames with deeply nicked edges, alternate with rubies, one of which has been lost. The brooch is probably fourteenth-century. (National Museum of Wales, Cardiff. Actual size.)

Plate 22 (left). Finger rings from ecclesiastical graves are a source of information about jewellery until the fifteenth century (see plates 4 and 9). This gold ring is from the grave of Henry Woodcock, Bishop of Winchester, who died in 1316. A large oval sapphire is held to the bezel by four claws, each of which is cut at the end into a fleur-de-lys. (In Winchester Cathedral. Photograph by the Victoria and Albert Museum. Actual size.)

Plate 23 (right). This ring was almost certainly also a bishop's, as it comes from Wells Cathedral, but unfortunately it is not known in whose grave it was found. The stone is a large octagonal amethyst, cut so that the top has three facets. As it is rare to find stones that have been so carefully cut, this ring has been compared to those from Durham (plate 4) and attributed to the twelfth century. The 'architectural' motif of the open cusped quatrefoil on the shoulders is more likely to date from the thirteenth or fourteenth century, however. It may be a twelfth-century gem reused in a later setting. (Now in the British Museum. Actual size.)

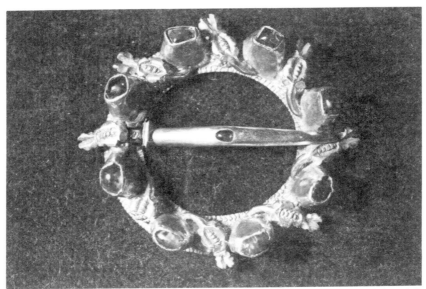

Plate 24. A very fine gold ring brooch of the thirteenth or fourteenth century. It has eight sapphires (one is missing) held in very high settings, from the base of each of which there grows a stem that opens out into a gold flower. There is another stone in the centre of the pin, which also has a bar across the hinge end, a common feature on such brooches (compare plate 7). Ring brooches with multiple stones in high settings were popular, and there are many base metal examples set with glass or paste instead of gems. (Manchester City Art Gallery. Twice actual size.)

Plate 25. Gold ring brooch (the pin missing). The frame is engraved with the names of the Three Kings, Jaspar, Melchior and Balthazar — the inscription was a protection against the falling sickness — a crown, and an M for Mary. It ends with a little spray of flowers. The brooch was found in King's Lynn, Norfolk, and is probably fourteenth-century. (Victoria and Albert Museum. 1½ times actual size.)

Plate 26 (left). This gold finger ring is called a *gimmel* ring (from the French word for twins). The paired bezel symbolises two lovers side by side. In this example the stones are a ruby and a turquoise. (British Museum. Twice actual size.)

Plate 27 (right). Another finger ring suitable as a gift to a loved one. The hoop is formed from a knot of twisted gold wires, symbolising lovers intertwined, and there are panels with the inscription *Pensez de moy* ('Think of me'). In the photograph, the last word is shown. The background was originally enamelled. The ring was found in Whitechapel, London, and the style of the lettering is a clue to its date, which is probably fourteenth-century. (British Museum. Twice actual size.)

Plate 28. One of the finest surviving pieces of medieval jewellery is the Founder's Jewel of New College, Oxford, presented by William of Wykeham in 1404. It is in the shape of a letter M, with a crowned top, for Mary, patron saint of the college; the gold figures are the Angel of the Annunciation and Mary, and on the central bar of the M is a gold fleur-de-lys, growing from a beautifully shaped ruby 'vase'. The other stones are pearls and emeralds. The lilies and the angel's wings are enamelled. The figures stand in an 'architectural' frame, with cusped trefoils at the tops (compare plate 23). Very fine beading divides the frame into panels. (New College, Oxford. Photograph by Victoria and Albert Museum. Actual size.)

Plate 29. King Richard II of England (1377-99) shown on a panel painted in the 1390s (opposite). The panel is one of a pair; the other shows the Christ Child with Mary, to whom Richard is paying homage. He is shown with three supporting patrons, St Stephen, St Edward the Confessor and St John the Baptist. The painting shows various different jewels in use. Richard is wearing a gold crown, decorated with pearls and coloured stones. Around his neck is a collar of broom-cods, the use of the broom plant probably being a symbol of English claims to lands in France. The pairs of broom-cods are joined together by link pieces studded with pearls, and there is a more elaborate link piece at the throat. Below the collar, Richard is wearing his personal badge, the chained white hart. The animal is lying down and has a gold crown and chain round its neck. The branches of its antlers end in small pearls, and the body was presumably covered with white enamel (compare plate 31). The same motifs, the chained hart and the broom-cods, can be seen on Richard's robes. St Stephen and St Edward are also shown with crowns; the former has a splendid brooch holding the hems of his robe together on his chest. St Edward is carrying a ring, probably an allusion to the ring which he was supposed to have presented to the shrine of St John the Baptist at Havering. The drawings (above) clarify details of the jewellery shown on the panel, which is now in the National Gallery, London.

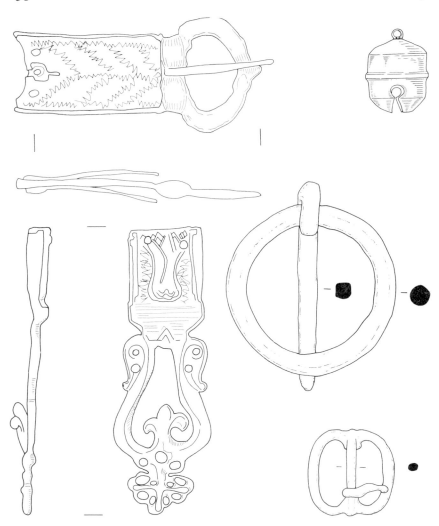

Plate 30. There was a wide variety of small bronze objects in everyday use in the middle ages. This selection shows a thirteenth-century or fourteenth-century buckle with a plate decorated with simple zigzag patterns; the leather strap would have been held by rivets at the end. Next to it is a late medieval 'rumbler' bell, which would have had an iron 'pea' inside it. Below that is a simple ring buckle, of the fourteenth or fifteenth century. Bottom left is an elaborate late medieval strap end, with a vase-like decoration on the plate into which the strap would have fitted. Finally there is double-frame or spectacle buckle, probably fifteenth-century. (All actual size.)

Plate 31. The Dunstable swan. This outstanding jewel was excavated in 1965 by the Manshead Archaeological Society on the site of the Dominican priory in Dunstable. It would have been worn as a badge which alluded to the story of the Swan Knight, from whom various noble families claimed descent, and whose motif was adopted by King Henry IV (1399-1412), becoming a badge of the Lancastrian cause in the fifteenth century (compare Richard II's white hart, plate 29). The jewel is made of gold, the swan's feathers being formed in white enamel. Round its neck is a coronet, to which is attached a miniature chain. The pin which held the jewel in place can be seen projecting behind the tail feather. The technique of all-over enamelling was introduced at the end of the fourteenth century, and this jewel was probably made in Paris at about that time. It might have come to England as a gift to the king or to one of his supporters, or one of them might have bought it in France. (British Museum. Actual size.)

Plate 32. Gold pendant, engraved with the Crucifixion, St John the Baptist with the Lamb of God, and a bishop, presumably Thomas à Becket. Sprays of leaves and flowers complete the pattern. The background has black enamel. The pendant would have been worn on a chain or as the centrepiece of a necklace. It demonstrates the conventional piety of the fourteenth and fifteenth centuries, when religious themes more often illustrated the Crucifixion, with its theme of mortality and man's earthly sins, than the protective formulae of earlier pieces (plate 25). The use of enamel as a background is also a feature of this later period. (Found at Matlaske, Norfolk. Now in Norwich Museum, Norfolk. Photograph by Victoria and Albert Museum. Actual size.)

Plate 33. The Clare cross. This fifteenth-century pendant was found at Clare Castle, Suffolk, and is owned by Her Majesty the Queen. The gold panel shows Christ crucified, wearing a loin cloth. There was originally enamel on the background, but this has fallen out, to reveal how the gold surface was roughened to make the enamel bind on to it better. The panel covers a cavity in which a tiny relic could be kept. There are pearls pinned into the angles of the cross; one on the side has fallen off. The ends of the cross are elaborately punched with scrolls and the letters *INRI* (for *Iesus Nazarenus Rex Iudeorum*), which also occur on the scroll across the top of the crucifix. (British Museum. Actual size.)

Plate 34. The Thame hoard. This collection of five gold rings was dredged out of a river near Thame, Oxfordshire, in 1940, with coins, of which the latest dates to about 1460. The hoard was probably lost at about that time — the objects may have been put in a bag or a box and hidden in the water by someone who never came back for them. Of the four smaller rings, the top row centre has a hexagonal peridot held in a claw setting. Its hoop is engraved with sprays of flowers (compare plate 32). Next to it is a plainer ring, with a toadstone (a fossilised tooth). On the bottom row is a stirrup-shaped ring with a turquoise (compare plates 15 and 16). Next to it is a ring which has no stone; it is a love ring, engraved with the inscription *Tout pour vous* ('All for you') and sprays of flowers. The largest ring holds an enormous amethyst, cunningly cut into a double-armed cross. This ring is also shown on the front cover, and details of it are on the opposite page. It probably dates from the late fourteenth or early fifteenth century, perhaps being of Burgundian workmanship. (Ashmolean Museum, Oxford. Actual size.)

Plate 35 (above left). Side view of the Thame ring, showing one of the seven amethysts on the hoop and how the bezel is a small rectangular casket for containing a relic (compare plate 33). An inscription, *Memanto mei Domine* ('Remember me O Lord'), starts on the top of the ring and continues round the side: in this picture the letter *E* and *D* are cut in openwork on the side of the bezel and there is an *I* on the left boss of the shoulder; the other boss has a crown engraved on it.

Plate 36 (above right). On the back of the Thame ring is engraved a Crucifixion scene (compare plate 33) with Christ, the sun and moon above him, and Mary and St John weeping beside him. The background is red enamel.

Plate 37. The projecting flowers on the ends of the casket are knobs which can be turned to unlock it. The top (right) and the amethyst cross (centre) can then be lifted out, revealing an unattached separate gold plate with a spray of flowers engraved on it (left), a motif which is also on the inside of the backplate of the casket (centre); the relic would have been held between the plate and the back.

Plate 38. Pilgrims wore badges on their hats to show which shrines they had visited. Usually made of lead, the badges often, as in these two examples, took the form of miniature flasks *(ampullae)* in which was water or oil blessed at the shrine. The upper drawing shows the two sides of an ampulla recently excavated at Portchester Castle, Hampshire. The crowned *W* shows that it came from the shrine of St Mary at Walsingham, Norfolk. The most famous English shrine was that of Thomas à Becket at Canterbury, from which came the ampulla in the lower drawing. On the flask is the Archbishop, with his right hand raised in blessing, and there is a complex openwork border with a Latin inscription around the edge, much of which is now missing, but which probably translated 'Thomas is the best healer of the holy sick'. (Actual sizes.)

Plate 39. Perhaps a near contemporary of the Thame ring (plates 34-7) and also ascribed to Burgundian workmanship is this gold finger ring. The shoulders are cut into dragons which grip the bezel in their jaws. The stone, an olivine, is held in a claw setting. The openwork quatrefoils round the side and the trefoil on the underside are in the 'architectural' tradition (compare plates 23 and 28). The open trefoil allowed the stone to come into contact with the wearer's finger, enhancing its protective properties. (Found at Alvechurch, Worcestershire. Birmingham City Museums. 1½ times actual size.)

Plate 40 (left). Gold finger ring called *iconographic* because it is engraved with religious themes. The centre of the three figures is Mary, holding the Christ Child, with St Helena beside her. Above these is a Crucifixion scene, with God the Father looking down upon Christ on the Cross. Not visible is an inscription engraved inside the hoop, *En bon an* ('Happy New Year'), showing that it was given as a New Year gift. (Ashmolean Museum, Oxford. 1½ times actual size.)

Plate 41 (right). Gold finger ring set with small stones. It has been suggested that the shape symbolises the Crown of Thorns, so that it would be another example of a fifteenth-century religious theme associated with the Crucifixion. Like the ring on plate 40, it has an inscription inside the hoop, *Whan yo loke on this, thynk on them yt* (that) *yave you this,* so it too was given as a present. (Found in the river Thames at Westminster. British Museum. 1½ times actual size.)

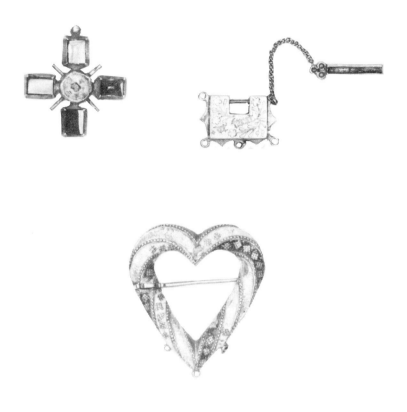

Plate 42. In 1966 a hoard of medieval jewellery was found at Fishpool, Nottinghamshire, together with over a thousand gold coins, the latest of which dated to 1461-4. This suggests that the hoard was deposited during the Wars of the Roses, like the Thame hoard (plates 34-7). The jewels were four gold finger rings (plate 46), two lengths of gold chain (plate 44) and four gold jewels (plates 42, 43 and 45), three of which are shown here. On the left is a pendant cross; it has four rectangular amethysts set in the arms, and a central stone is missing. The pins in the angles of the cross were probably for pearls (compare plate 33). Next to it is a unique discovery, a miniature gold padlock with its key linked to it by a small chain. It is engraved with flowers and an inscription, which was filled with white enamel for contrast (see plate 43). Below is a heart-shaped brooch, set with beading to give it a spiral effect and enamelled white and blue, in which tiny spots of gold are 'floating'. (British Museum. Actual size.)

Plate 43. The reverse side of the three jewels from Fishpool shown on plate 42. The pendant cross has a central ruby held in a claw setting, and each of the four arms is engraved with an eight-petalled flower. The reverse of the miniature padlock has sprays of flowers like those on the front and the rest of the inscription, *De tout mon cuer* ('With all my heart') — a text like those on love rings (plate 27), which was perhaps chosen to imply that the donor's heart was locked to his true love. The key actually works; when pushed down a slot in the side of the padlock, it releases the bar. The jewel can thus be worn as the centrepiece of a necklace, holding the ends of a gold chain together (see plate 44). The loops on the side were probably to hold dangling pearls or other small stones. The back of the brooch has a text appropriate for its shape, *Je suy vostre sans de partier* — 'I am yours alone' (literally 'without sharing'). As on the padlock, the inscription was enamelled in white, and there are sprays of flowers with it. (British Museum. Actual size.)

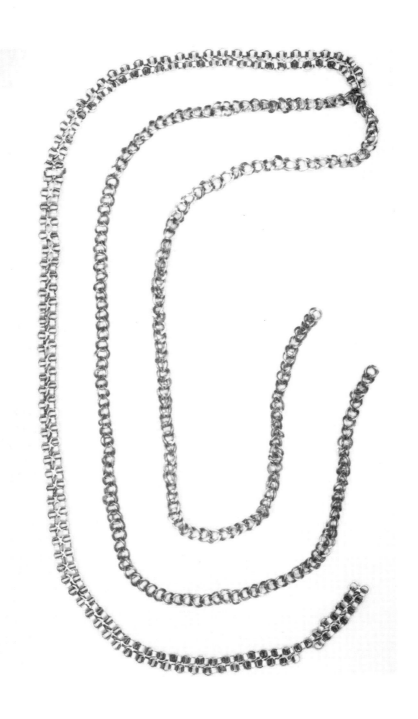

Plate 44 (opposite). There were two chains in the Fishpool hoard, which had been linked together. One has figure-of-eight links, one ovals. Such chains were worn with pendants (plates 32, 33, 45), shorter lengths being worn with, for instance, badges (plate 31). The lengths are $21\frac{1}{4}$ inches (540 mm) and $12\frac{1}{4}$ inches (311 mm). (British Museum.)

Plate 45. The fourth jewel in the Fishpool hoard is a small pendant roundel, three views of which are shown here. On the front (left) is a sapphire in a claw setting, surrounded by beads of white enamel, many of which are missing. There is a very delicate band of goldwork, and the outer edge is serrated. The back of the roundel (right) is engraved with a six-petalled flower, perhaps intended as a badge of the house of Lancaster. There are loops for pendant stones. The roundel may be of Flemish workmanship. (British Museum. Actual size.)

Plate 46. The final photograph of the Fishpool hoard shows the four gold finger rings found in it. Top left is a shape which was used almost throughout the middle ages (see plates 9, 15 and 16). There is a turquoise in the claw setting. Next to it is a very worn iconographic ring, which has a figure engraved on the bezel, perhaps a bishop with his mitre (compare plate 40). Its condition implies that it was quite old when deposited. Below left is a signet ring, engraved with the device of a hawk's lure and fleurs-de-lys. It is not known whose seal this was. There are flowers engraved on the shoulder. Last is a band of gold, beaded on the outside to look as though it is a spiral. On the inside is an inscription in English, *Uphaf ye entier,* with a heart between the last two words ('Lift up your whole heart'). It has been suggested that this is a translation from a Latin verse used in the Mass, so that the ring would have a religious text. (British Museum. Actual size.)

Index